1

Bible Land Blues

Jacob Rabinowitz

dedicated to
Aharon Amir
poet, patriot, Canaanite,
friend to me where friends were very few

Prologue

I knew it was no answer to stare down the Bible, reading a page-flip animated cartoon of the past —

Yet still, it was a portal, an entrance —

For the center, the place where the three worlds (Heaven, Earth and Sheol) meet, was also here.

The holy book opened on the world of the dead. Its scholars weren't just unsunned library-pale, but wan with pouring heart's blood and life's time down the hellmouth of the past, drink-offering for the shadows that squeak their memories, flickering in and out of existence even as they speak, like frames in a silent movie or like you feel after too much coffee.

I made a last hero's descent into this land of the dead — a Hebrew initiatory ordeal — to wrest from the ghosts their secrets. I dug deep, beyond the time of the Bible itself, into the Canaanite and Near Eastern past which underlay it. These points of contact with Near Eastern mythology constitute the Earthly Sophia who "played before the Lord and was his darling and delight." They were the exuberant, image-rich spiritual earth under Yahweh's unimaginable heaven, the archetypes of ancient Canaan that had survived as extravagant metaphors in the prophets and renewed a fantastic and equivocal existence in the Kabbalah. These were the ground, both ontologically and physically, of Jewish spirituality.

And the ground is exactly what is at issue. We already experience the world primarily through the windshield or the television screen and risk becoming science fiction brains-in-a-jar, devotees of Our Lady of the Immaculate Perception, clicking the TV remote control as a rosary. But by restoring the Canaanite mythology, the soul of the recovered land, I meant to become, in a sense, the first spiritual Zionist, mixing a "cup of staggering" from Baal and the Baal Shem Tov.

There was nowhere left to go but Israel itself to make an attempt to reanimate the vision in the place it first arose. It was to be the *Alchemy of the Word* and Abyssinia all in one. It was a disaster.

But this is the chronicle of my attempt to reconquer the Holy Land.

Bible Land Blues

I

The Night Journey

Glory to the one who transported his servant by
   night . . .

Surely I have attained the condition of spirits:
the whole world's width between home and here
flown in a night, a dream, a prolonged thought.

Did the mountains flatten, the valleys rise,
the three dimensions condense to two
that I skimmed across them,
glib as a fingertip over a map?

Time's annihilated:
my thirty-six years packed in thirteen boxes;
a lifetime's accidents suddenly pattern
around the single fact
of return, of ascension to this state,
this condition of Israel.

II

Surface Mail

In America, Israel was a map on my wall,
a page of Bible, a newspaper headline,
a star-chart whose constellations
were the Hebrew alphabet —
the swastika, a terrible comet-like Aleph.

I've mailed myself into the text:
the proof is the photo on my ID card,
Israel's seal stamped on my face
like a heavenly postmark.

Flattened by the weight of Diaspora,
I slip easily into the envelope,
drop on a desk in the Ministry of Immigration
like foreign mail from the nineteenth century,
 a thin, implausible arrival
speaking the language as learned from Prayerbook
and Bible — King James Hebrew,

and unequal to this life in three dimensions,
inadequate before the white stone riddling the
    hills
around Jerusalem, gathered into strata, tier on tier,

slope-side crop-shelves of the farming Canaanites.

What message can I bring the shaggy columnar
    palms,
the broad goose-bumped paddles of the cactus,
the close-up foliage immediately green?

With a cold mercy, it begins to rain.
Jerusalem becomes a stone fountain,
every outdoor stairs a waterfall,
streets ankle deep.
As the white mist permits, Jerusalem's traffic,
stones and foliage
dissolve into Yahweh.

III

The World-to-Come

Proverb of the Diaspora:
"When you're in love, the whole world looks
    Jewish."
Here, I am, evidently, in love:
the late winter mist around me is a nimbus
of indistinct affection for my fellow Israelites.

At the bus stop, a woman who looks like my
    grandmother.
I stare, sucking the small and personal pang
like a cut finger.

These streets are full of my dead relatives,
drawn from the black well of the underworld,
the silver waters of the gene-pool.

Surely this is the World-to-Come
where the dead return, where men have wings —
around me a flock of tourists descends
to peck at falafels, flutter their coats
and chirp in German.

IV

Spring

Skyward spray of wildflowers,
delicate fireworks of yellow, white and red
almost reaching your knees. You stand
above them, peering down like a surprised
    giantess.

You name the flowers for me in Hebrew:
Nurit, Cochvan, Dam Maccabeem —
I try the words in my mouth
like exotic fruit I'm not sure how to eat.

And Jacob served seven years for Rachel
and they seemed to him but a few days,
for the love he had to her . . .

and you're lying on the grass and your neck
is the same timeless white as the stones of Judea
which shone as now when Jacob first
saw his pale Rachel and those seven years
blanched into one nightless day.

You sit up, frown at me writing this,
begrudge the little heat my notebook's shadow

steals from the day. But I promise

an autumn evening to come
when you'll read by lamplight
what I now write in sunlight
and remember April's warmth in the season of
    rains.

V

I Am That I Am

Map of the Holy Land, of *Terra Sancta:*
Sodom flames in the south;
eastward Babel towers;
in the center, Jerusalem, a perfect circle.

Truer than modern geography
to the spirit of this emphatic land,
this strip of sand set beside the rest of the middle
    east
like an exclamation point at the end of a phrase —
to indicate stress —

for surely some important thing is shown
in the bees big as birds, the weeds like trees,
terrific thistles, a nightmare of spikes,
from which the armored Crusaders,
the clanking Franks, could perhaps have hacked
bouquets. And something momentous, essential,
is said by the buffeting sunlight, the carhorns,
the shoving onto busses, the barking dogs,
the babies howling insistent as existence;
Israel, like her God, says, "I am, I still am," —

all her history and prophecy
one relentless conjugation of the verb "to be."

I listen like the true and antique pilgrim
with beard and staff on the corner of my Latin
    map,
like him I add my "praise ye the Lord"
to these rude Hallelujahs.

VI

I Don't Understand, I Say Yes

So far a thousand words, some the same as in
    English —
like raisins in the bread of Hebrew,
so far an impossible Christmas list
of words to memorize on bus rides.

My thoughts struggle out in the words I know —
ill-fitting, ridiculous clothes.
Someone is telling me some rapid thing.
I don't understand. I say yes.

These days I'm always at someone's door,
a welcome — well at least a surprise.
I'm like a man who fell out of the sky
(which, in a manner of speaking, I did).
I wish I could be as wise as my silence,
instead I re-read the letter from home
and kiss the signature. Did I expect different?
I don't understand. I say yes.

My head is full of what I can't speak,
the bus-stop is full of girls I can't joke with,

in uniform, younger and braver than me.
Unpatriotically I just want to cry.
Do you know what that's like?
If you don't understand, just say yes.

VII

Jerusalem

for Yehuda Amichai

i

A coin with the seal of the Jewish kingdom
in the hand of a Jerusalem beggar
looks for an instant like a royal ring
turned 'round on the finger so the bezel faces in.
The ring on the hand of the disguised Messiah
asking alms at the gate, as in Talmudic legend?
Once. Now it's the hand of Jerusalem
accepting the small change of Tourism.

ii

Jerusalem's a city of the dead —
the cemeteried slopes of the Mount of Olives
are the least of it. Zion's rebuilders
stack the land with granite
as pilgrims lay stones on the grave of a saint.

Once the Hollywood of world religions,
she's become the old folks' home of world
    scriptures
— the Dead Sea Scrolls in their intensive-care
    shrine
are the least of it.

iii

And you're the garrulous poetic sheriff
of this ghost-town in the Judaean desert,
You're drunk with history, and like all drunks,
like all history, you repeat yourself,
grandmother stories, newspaper headlines,
neighborhood gossip and popular songs —
if we weren't here you'd talk to the Wall.

An out-of-work prophet in the capitol,
dead center, of a dreamy Mythuania,
crooning over the graves
of extinct relationships.

The man who's lost his faith in God
believes in death, and women.

iv

Jerusalem looks always east, sadly
trying to see past the Wailing Wall:
that rampart is the limit of history,
each stone an implacable fact,
a brick of tradition sealing this ghetto
of second-hand time.

Traditionally, pious visitors
write out requests on slips of paper
then slide their folded prayers
into the chinks between the stones —
it's desperate, the way they caulk the Wall,
as if they saw it beginning to leak.
What terrible flood does the wall keep back,
what pagan Euphrates?

Jerusalem's air is a smog of sorrow,
polluted with prayers, misty with nostalgia.
Not even the new and high hotels
rise out of this fog for all their ugliness,
not even they can see over the Wall
that looms through time, shadowing the town
into a twilight where Mother Tradition
says: "Rest your head on my sagging breasts,
eat my Sabbath table's challah bread,

21

golden and braided like the hair of Asherah,
the Canaanite goddess of Love."

VIII

Tel Aviv

Jerusalem's a Diaspora dream,
familiar. In Tel Aviv, by the sea,
you first realize that "there" is now here,
giddily feel the distance down-planet
to where you once were.
Who stands in Tel Aviv
stands in Israel, is precipitously *here*
in the Promised Land, the pagan Canaan,
under Shamash the sun-god,
Yareyak the Moon,
and El, lord of the stars.

Tel Aviv faces the sea,
the fluid future, the West.
Tel Aviv is the city of the ocean-god Yam,
the palace of the water-dragon Leviathan,
whose waters coil and uncoil at her feet,
each wave a scale with a crescent edge of foam.
The wind in these streets is the breath of sea,
smelling like chaos, like salt, like sex.

IX

Prayer to the New Moon

We're a people who count our months by the
    moon,
change is in our nature. Why weep
for Jerusalems real or imagined?
The sea of Time where Judaism sank
cast up Tel Aviv and the Canaanite myths
recovered from the ruins of ancient Ugarit.

Thirty-six years of changing moons
have already passed over my head;
my hair begins to silver, altered and conformed
to the moonbeams that have touched it.

Yareyak, the moon, goddess of changes,
pulls us as she does the tides,
with every pulse she tugs our blood,

flesh ebbs, bones blanch
white as shells,
as the ruins of Jericho,
"City of the Moon,"

X

The Happy Birthday of Death

In Canaanite religion, the round of the seasons figured forth an ever-repeating cyclic history of the gods. Every summer Mot, the god of death and drought, killed Baal, the god of life and rainfall. Thereupon, as the July heat set in, the Canaanite sky-god El would retire to Har Tsaphon, a mountain in Syria, the Canaanite Olympus, to escape the rigors of the Israeli summer, and Mot had undisputed mastery of the earth.

Baal would, of course, return to life when the autumn rains came, but his "death" was signalized by ritual mourning at the height of summer. Similar myths and observances are recorded for the entire middle east, as, for example, for Baal's cognate gods Adonis and Tammuz.

Rabbinic Judaism reinterpreted this ancient and ineradicable holiday as a fast day to commemorate the destruction of Jerusalem by Babylon in 587 B.C. on the ninth of Av (the Hebrew month which corresponds to July-August).

When the day becomes one long soundless thud
of sun, and motion is madness
under light's white weight, the punishing summer
when El abandons Israel for his mountain in the
    north,

when the land is blanching and spring's
    wildflowers
have burned away like a colored haze,
leaving only the butane-blue thistle —
memorial candle for the death of Baal,

when "the whole world languisheth and fadeth
    away"
dead wood silvers in the bleaching beams,
chalk-dusty stone shines dry as shell
in a landscape glaring like a shoreless beach

and the overhead blue has become Mot's ocean,
dead clear and perfect, implacable sapphire
where Shamash, the sun-god, unendurable star
rules a view that shimmers mistlessly
    and glimmers without dew,

then day's night-quiet, and twilight's the dawn
of lamplit parties in the dark and cool:
Mot, in evening clothes, drinks Tequila
in a Tel Aviv café and toasts the Ninth of Av.

XI

Gehenna

Gehenna is the Hell of Jewish legend: the name comes from the Hebrew for "Valley of the sons of Hinnom" — a small ravine to the southeast of the Old City of Jerusalem, now a park.

Friends of my parents visited, took me out
to a French retaurant, *Mishkanot Sha'ananim,*
expensively overlooking the Valley of Hinnom
where the Canaanites burned babes for Moloch
and the Hebrew kingdom buried its wealthier
    dead.

When, if not our heavens, at least our earth
was "rolled up like a scroll", became the Torah's
portable world, Gehenna flamed
for sinners.

           Nowadays the Hebrew Hell's
a public garden, and in its midst
the Cinemathèque remains infernally open
even on Shabbat, to offer Jerusalem
visions of the world of the dead:
movie stars of fifty years ago

appear as in life, flattened on the screen
as though pressing their faces eagerly against
the windows of this world.

        Tranquil,
several hundred meters above the green
and pleasant hell, myself something less
than a hundred shekels above destitution,
I stare out at Judah's bare hills,
clear skies, filled with my unsaleable visions.

XII

Tristia ex Judaea

End of August, first cool nights:
the heat fades like anger,
leaving an exhausted earth beneath
a sky that at last forgives this land,
as I do not.

For all its noise, a speechless land,
for all its life, a dead one;
for all its wars, a land at peace
with all it's failed to be.

XIII

Exilarch

My friends, ready for every adventure
back in drunken high-school nights,
traded it in for a mammal reality:
parmesan baby-puke stiff on their shoulder,
furniture, vacations and the will of the wife
whose thighs are the arch of Woman's final
    triumph
over a man and his dreams.

I alone am escaped to tell thee
if only because I fucked up every chance
to become the slave of pleasant circumstance.

I've kept, if nothing else, *my* dream —
of time lived vivid, mythic, rich,
deepened with meaning, where accidents pattern
and days have shape, where stories are valid
as maps of the world.

        And so, this furnished room,
toy shop of the gods,
filled with clay statues of Asherah
I sell to tourists, books, papers, teacups,

29

unperformed plays, unpublished poems,
unanswered mail — cascade of papers,
like the bureaucracy of some small, proud,
    forgotten,
independent Balkan state
too tiny to appear on any map —
my rented realm, my Mythuanian embassy
in mid-Jerusalem issuing poems
as passports to pagan, imaginal Canaan.

Here I live, like Lenin in Zurich,
wondering, while my hairline recedes,
how long till my losses are too great
(or too silly) for any revolution to redeem?

XIV

Days of Awe

The "Days of Awe" are the holidays Rosh HaShannah (New Year) and Yom Kippur (a day of fasting and repentance). These observances correspond temporally and symbolically to the Canaanite myth and ritual which marked the return to life of Baal and the onset of the Autumn rains, at which time he, the storm-god, "wedded" the earth.

In Canaan, as thoroughout the ancient middle east, a sacred marriage rite celebrated these events: the king, representing the storm-god, copulated with the high priestess, who stood for the goddess of earth and fertility. Their union would magically encourage the sky to fertilize the earth with his rain.

The Hebrew prophets, who borrowed largely from Canaanite myth and poetry, did not omit this striking bit of religious theater: the prophet Hosea was commanded by God to marry a whore in order to symbolize God's enduring romantic commitment to Israel, who had "played the whore" with foreign gods. In chapter two of Hosea, Yahweh describes his final reconciliation with Israel, which the prophet's marriage has mimed, in terms that explicitly invoke the Canaanite rite — Yahweh promises Israel he will "sow

31

his seed in her in the land," with verbal elaborations on the theme that are by turns erotic and agricultural. One phrase from this rather awesome, and sometimes geographical, declaration of love has found a very prominent place in the daily ritual of Rabbinic Judaism: the placing and binding on the arm of Tefillin.

Tefillin are black leather cubes containing parchments inscribed with verses from scripture. They are equipped with long leather straps and worn on the forehead and the left arm by orthodox Jews during morning prayer. The strap of the arm-tefillin is wound seven times around the forearm and then looped around the ring-finger of the left hand. While this last action is performed one recites the verse Erastik li l'olam, *"I betrothe thee to me forever" the formula of marriage between God and Israel from Hosea 2: 21.*

Resurrection

The long dry heat went thick with mist.
September's end.

        The sweat-slick body of the god
bandaged in soaking clothes lies,
an unalive Osiris in its oblong box,
a hotel room in downtown Haifa,
airless and cheap.

Yom Kippur. Busy Haifa stifles
under its heat and its religion.
The streets are eerily empty,
and deader than Shabbat in Jerusalem.
Baal, in his coffin, turns the pillow
drier side up, slips uneasily
back into uneven sleep.

Sunset. In the synagogues they sing
the *Ne'ilah*, the closing prayer
of the Yom Kippur service,
as Baal, curled around an erotic dream
sprays his belly with fertilizing rain
and the first cool wind since Spring
blows in off the sea, lifting the heat.

Baal wakes, gulps the last wine
in the bedside bottle,
goes out to look for the whore Israel.

ii

Sacred Marriage

He found her, flat on her back in an alley.
a long piece of cardboard for a mattress,
fucking some immigrant drunk for fifty sheckels.

(This was the poet Rabinovich who,
recognizing the god — poets are still capable
of such piety — lifted himself

from the prostrate nation, readjusted his clothes,
implausibly elegant
as a homeless cat grooming itself on a dumpster.)

The lovers rejoined went back to her concrete
cell of an apartment where she tied up
with gesture so deft as could only come
of 2,000 years of laying tefillin.

Baal held the syringe, and as he pressed
the smack-rich blood back down her vein
he whispered *"Erastik li l'olam."*

Then when opiates had given Israel back
at least the feel of immortality,
she was bold to ask "Will you really be my
    boyfriend?

take me to movies? You really don't mind
that I got fat?" Baal, touching her lips
with a divine finger, says "Shhhhhhhh . . ."

XV

Oy

At the end of the Jewish Sabbath
a many-wicked candle is extinguished
in a cup of wine: this is called *havdallah:*
it breaks the spell of the seventh day
and marks the resumption of vulgar time.

Once Shamash plunged his solar torch
into the western sea, *havdallah* of the gods,
beginning not a week but an age

in which an old-new people hurries
to forget its past, erecting around itself
not, as St. John envisaged,
the New Jerusalem, not yet as Aharon Amir
exults, the New Rome — it's more like the second
New Jersey —

At the edge of Haifa they're bulldozing the last
fine examples of Ottoman architecture
to build a mall. In the Ministry of Immigration
they're demolishing the last fine example
of Zionist idealism. "What are you, a child?

Do we have to do everything for you?
You don't even have the form.
You'll have to come back tomorrow at 2
(when I won't be here)."

I have three degrees, I speak ten languages,
I'm almost forty, thirty-nine apartments
wouldn't rent to me because I'm a dirty
    immigrant.
"What do you want *me* to do about it?"

In Israel, they know how to treat you like a Jew.

I'm staring at nothing, pouring Arak
down my guts to cauterize my existential wounds,
to throw another jolt through my bloated sick
    liver,
to write in poet's blood, most indelible of inks,
for a sign above your gates,
upon the doorposts of your houses

Aliyah Macht Frei.

Looking down from Mt. Carmel, through the haze,
shore-sky-land all blend, vague and bright —
not even Shamash can separate the realms.

November returns with the mist which is life,
and nothing in life is all that clear . . .

XVI

The Great Resurrection

December. Baal keeps running windy fingers
over Carmel's curves, flogging back the trees.
He moans, and loud, and for days on end.
Someone's shutter bangs bangs bangs
in inanimate copulation.
"It's too cold," says Asherah, the sleeping earth,
"not *now* . . . "

Unlike Baal, I do believe Spring will return,
and unlike Adonai, I'm no longer intrigued by
    Belief.

The State of Israel doesn't coincide
with my *condition* of Israel
which is realized, it seems in motion alone,
mapless as desire,
existing by instants, furtive as a glance,
tho' ready to steal itself some realness,
an Israel whose scriptures are innocent
as a dirty joke, and truthful as travelers' tales.

I glimpsed it yesterday — the sea was windless,

the sea Baal's been whipping white all month,
now still as though time itself had stopped
under sunset gold of incandescing cloud-edge
(*my* wealth — fairy gold and temporary gems).
I looked and looked, stupid and lucid,
for a moment and finally arrived.

XVII

For now, it's cold . . .

This killing Winter damp has touched the bone
through flesh, through sweater, and through
   countless cups
of tea, through pastures worth of knitted wool
and steaming leagues of tea; still cold, I lean
above the heater, palms out, dreamy, dull.

The Winter rain seeps down grave-deep. The souls
whose bodies are dissolving in the dirt
swim clear and downward, slowly peopling   ·
the earth's unending dream. Ereshkigal,
the queen of Under-earth, black Asherah,
the kindly one, accepts them with her vast
and necessary love, rejecting none.

Oh when it's warm again I'll face the world,
recording angels of the TV news,
the frightened Arabs and we frightened Jews,
our backs against the wall, the Wailing Wall,

unhappy soldiers. When it's warm again
I'll think it through, or maybe let it fade
to vagueness on the beach of Tel Aviv

where college kids, the Uzis on their backs
forgotten, eat ice-cream, inhabiting
the fragile California of an hour,
TV unreal and sweet as magazines,
imaginal America . . .

XVIII

Shalom

It's like when you no longer are in love
with someone — for the first time you can see
just what they really look like — man, that's cold!

The landscape grows opaque and flat — the shops
I'll never enter more, the friends I see
this last time, faces sad as photographs
and just as silent. Nothing more to say.
I'm guest at my own absence, shaking hands
and turning, heading off I don't know where.

I've no more stars of David in my eyes;
they knocked *that* nonsense out of me, long since.
I'd watch the girls on busses — like the girls
in ads — their smiles weren't meant for me.

Inanna, Sumer's Asherah, once tried
to seize control of Hell, the kingdom of Ereshkigal,
her sister: to extend the realm
of Love and of Fertility
beyond the grave, and to abolish death.

But entering the seven gates of Hell

she had to yield successively her clothes,
her ornaments, her pride, until she stood
all naked — as a corpse is naked — dead.

Inanna-like, I left at every step
(from customs to the unemployment line)
some level of my being: family,
friends, language, dignity — without complaint
I stripped, as for the doctor, stripped away
my Judaism, Zionism — flayed,

the wind of history blows cool across
the bones of this as yet unburied man
who stands as Moses stood on Pisgah, saw
far off the land that would be Israel, land
that he could never enter. There he died.
He scanned the people's future, I their past,
a palimpsest of glowing Torah spread
unfurled below, its time transformed to space,
a patterned animated Israel map
done on a scale of one-to-one —
sometimes
it coincides with this endangered strip
of shore-front middle-east, but mostly not.

My gods, they failed me. Baal became a drunk
and Asherah a prostitute, the realm
a room, the books I hadn't sold as yet
for bread, a loneliness as big as all

I saw when I looked out to sea —
out there's Marseilles,
the bigger sea, America,
indifferent El, off in his stupid clouds.
And Yahweh, he's the sum of all of this.

Israel, I loved you as a man can love
his future, pitied you like my own past.
I learned to be a Jewish Arab here,
slave labor, public property. Two years!
Two years and still my Hebrew's out of books —
so few of you would even speak to me!

I ghosted through here,
an invisible man
wandering across an empty land
and talking to himself

                                    . . in a dead language.

One message more I'll broadcast into space,

one further valentine into the void,

yet useless, yet at last the final word

of one who won't return — peace be within these
    gates

I could not enter, in God's name *shalom*.

It's night, and I'll be going soon. At night
we all left Egypt. Leaving is an art
the Jew has mastered.

                          That I came –
an error. But like all the great mistakes
I've made in life, I made this out of love —
my love of Jacob's race. Some comfort, that.

Epilogue

From Chaldee Ur to Tel Aviv
we've counted our months by the moon, Israel,
watched the zodiac's circling stars.
But since we viewed earth from moon
the many flat lands curved into one planet,
all outer space became our sky —

we had no map or calendar more,
the scriptures suddenly looked their age.

We have indeed "been made like the stars of heaven,"
like them we ride this horizonless dark . . .

Where now? In exile everywhere, my kingdom is the ancient books and a wandering among peoples who can have no love for my visions. Like Jeremiah in Egypt, I have nothing left but the grandeur of my failure, and it is of this I speak, if only to myself, and perhaps to God, who, if he doesn't listen, at least doesn't annoy me with advice.

He doesn't have to — I did nothing wrong — I'm not like Rimbaud, asking pardon for eating myself sick on lies, and ready to get modern with a penitent's zeal. Like Jeremiah, or better still, like Job, I protest my innocence with a neck unbent.

So I'm returned to the outer darkness of diaspora.
I don't live anywhere, does anyone live anywhere?

Airplane travel flattens every land to an
unmountained map, two dreary dimensions, and
distances measured not in miles but in money, and
when you get where you're going, you're still
where you were — same highway, junk food, pop
music —we've achieved a fast-paced frightful
immobility:
after 2,000 years it might as well still be the Roman
empire — everywhere aqueduct, forum,
amphitheater, every little town laid out exactly the
same, every language flattened under Latin.

For us its the highway, that most Roman road,
the suburb, most nowhere of places lawn-lined
avenues curling endless and repetitive, green
sprawl of inane paisley, or the uniform grid of city
streets, all roads leading to Rome . . . who needs a
map or calendar? — there's only one day, the
work-day, and only one place, without an
elsewhere.

Though speeding makes you feel you're going somewhere
all roads just lead to where you'll wait to pay.
In the global market sameness there is neither here nor there
and no place left that's sacred or profane.

When the highway and the mall are all in all,
one world of plastic,

48

one styrofoam whitened wave,
one high-speed immobility where supersonic transit
still dumps you in some ersatz USA . . .

It's the destination makes the road become the real, the path become the place —to where the world realigns around us, every direction radiating equidistant off, then the vision, then the *overview*.

This is the *Invitation to the Voyage*, the Caravan leaving, the pathway back about to vanish like incense on the wind, the long distance call — will you accept the charges? take the stand, and by your facing proclaim there *is* direction?

How many miles to Jerusalem? Is it further away than China, than childhood? Can I get you there by candle light?

Will you follow your nostalgia to the place that's really yours? Will you come away with me now while everyone's asleep?

Listen, every town, every house must be a model of the world, a 3-D mandala, radiating from a core soul-white and burning. In a City, that center is a garden, a palace, a temple: in every house, it's the hearth. But they made the city center an auto intersection, a mere convergence of roads, not one of them a Path. Where the world-tree had been planted, they pitched a church steeple, shadow-shrine of

49

their death-tree. In every house where the hearth should be they placed the cold blue fires of the TV screen — schlock portal on an underworld of spirits who try to sell you things . . .

Nor do I suggest you make the trip to Israel; I've been there, and even Jerusalem isn't necessarily Jerusalem . . .

If it isn't here, it's nowhere. *Therefore* it must be here.

The center, the point of pilgrimage, the crossroads, could it be wherever our paths cross, is it easy as our meeting? Few the places, few the times, you'll literally see the lights you'd call Jerusalem's flaring beyond the horizon like dawn seeping through a dream, when you'll hear it far off, homesick music in the wind,

> beyond the roar of traffic
> and every angry voice,
> can you hear the Levites singing,
> sad as man and strange as angel
> and as lonely as a choice?

It may be all we can do for now is remember she exists — and Rome wants nothing more than for you to forget. Remember! be it no more than a *mizrahi* on the wall, three stones heaped ziggurat-wise, a prayer said facing east . . . from a a hilltop, a rooftop, a prayer-rug, its patterns a map of where you are right now under heaven, an alignment with the place the realms interpenetrate. . .

"If I forget thee O Jerusalem . . . "

Point of origin, first land risen from the chaos-flood, still radiating the power of that *strong time*, of all places on earth the oldest, and the newest and the highest and the best.

Made in the USA
Las Vegas, NV
29 April 2021

22191273R00032